It Takes a Village Idiot...
and I Married one!

by Lois Pewterschmidt Griffin

**Helped into print by ALEX BORSTEIN
and CHERRY CHEVAPRAVATDUMRONG**

Based on the show created by SETH MACFARLANE

HARPER ● ENTERTAINMENT

NEW YORK · LONDON · TORONTO · SYDNEY

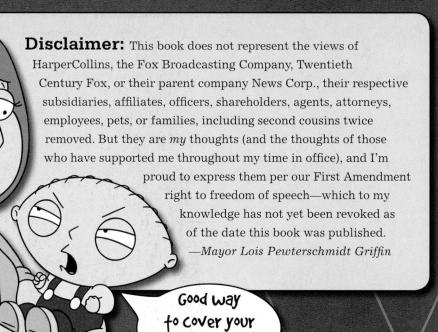

Disclaimer: This book does not represent the views of HarperCollins, the Fox Broadcasting Company, Twentieth Century Fox, or their parent company News Corp., their respective subsidiaries, affiliates, officers, shareholders, agents, attorneys, employees, pets, or families, including second cousins twice removed. But they are *my* thoughts (and the thoughts of those who have supported me throughout my time in office), and I'm proud to express them per our First Amendment right to freedom of speech—which to my knowledge has not yet been revoked as of the date this book was published.

—*Mayor Lois Pewterschmidt Griffin*

Good way to cover your publisher's ass.

HARPER ✦ ENTERTAINMENT

FAMILY GUY: IT TAKES A VILLAGE IDIOT . . . AND I MARRIED ONE! Copyright © 2007 by Twentieth Century Fox Film Corporation. All rights reserved. Printed in the United States of America. No part of this book may be used or reproduced in any manner whatsoever without written permission except in the case of brief quotations embodied in critical articles and reviews. For information address HarperCollins Publishers, 10 East 53rd Street, New York, NY 10022.

HarperCollins books may be purchased for educational, business, or sales promotional use. For information please write: Special Markets Department, HarperCollins Publishers, 10 East 53rd Street, New York, NY 10022.

FIRST EDITION

Designed by Timothy Shaner, nightanddaydesign.biz

Printed on acid-free paper

Library of Congress Cataloging-in-Publication Data is available upon request.

ISBN: 978-0-06-114332-8   ISBN-10: 0-06-114332-4

07 08 09 10 11 ✦/QBT 10 9 8 7 6 5 4 3 2 1

Contents

Preface

When HarperCollins first approached me to write an account of my time in office as Mayor of Quahog, I immediately asked how much money were they going to pay me. Their first offer seemed low, so I did some fishing around and found out what Hillary got paid for her book. Holy crap! I had no idea how lucrative this could be. I went back to HarperCollins and demanded a ridiculous amount of money and they actually met me halfway, so here goes nothin'.

#23-2146

HARPER

Pay to the Order of ___Lois Pewterschmidt Griffin___ $1,000,000

___One Million___ Dollars

Memo: ___For telling it all!___

Harper Collins

⊏19957659 25447617 23-2146

vi

Introduction

My time in office as Mayor of Quahog was one of the best periods of my life, one I will always look back on fondly. (**It's right up there next to my honeymoon, my bachelorette party, and my brief adventures as a lesbian during my sophomore year at college.**) I will forever be proud of the fact that, as mayor, I was able to take a small amount of control into my own hands—that I was able to restore some of our government's original intentions as laid out by our founding fathers so long ago. It seems as if our leaders, of late, are running away with our country, or trying to anyway. They have spied on civilians, leaked secret information to the public to better their own political agenda, and have sent our sons and daughters into a war we shouldn't be fighting. One of my goals while in office was to try to return to the practice of democracy that our great country was built upon. To once again exercise the muscles that Alexis de Tocqueville so admired. What waited for me in office were many lessons—some of which I had to learn the hard way. The first and most important lesson I learned was that it takes much more than one person to make an impact.

From the very first day of my campaign I knew I couldn't win without the help of the great people of Quahog. More specifically, I knew that I couldn't do it without the help of my family and dear friends. And now that it's time to write these memoirs, **I know that because I didn't get to the mayor's office alone, I don't have the right to tell the tale of my time there alone either.** So I share the next 100 pages of this book with the people who put me in office—the people without whom I'd still just be a mother and housewife. (Not that those jobs are any easier, mind you, but you get the idea.)

Chapter 1
Lois Pewterschmidt Griffin, My Living History

I was twelve years old when I found out I was rich. Growing up in Newport, everyone was well-off, so it wasn't until we took a trip to New York City that I really understood what a huge disparity there was between the wealthy and the poor. My parents and I were walking out of Radio City Music Hall where we had just seen the Rockettes in their Christmas Show. Daddy was talking about how beautiful the dancers' legs were and how my mother had really "let herself go," when we happened upon a homeless man. The man looked as if he were in his forties, and he wore an old, filthy coat with tattered sleeves. As we passed, he extended his grimy hand, palm up, and begged, "Spare some change, Sir?" I remember looking up at my father as he reached into his front trouser pocket, fumbling for some change. **After a moment, my father pulled his empty hand out of his pocket and flipped the beggar the bird saying, "Bite me, ya' hobo!"** On the car ride home, Mother explained to me that there are two types of people in the world: those with money and those who are just filthy and lazy.

That summer I went to sleep-away camp for the first time. It was at the Park Barrington Hotel in Newport and we were really roughing it. Maid service came only once every other day. I shared my room with a girl named Sharon Hendricks, who was accepted to the camp on scholarship. She was middle-class, but very pretty. I will never forget some of the important life lessons I learned from Sharon that summer. I learned that most people don't have hundreds of thousands of dollars in liquid assets. I learned that lower-income girls got their periods earlier. I learned that "Labia Majora" was not the name of a character in *Private Benjamin*. But most importantly, I learned that, money wasn't everything, and that most people in the world are good people just trying to get by.

A Word from
CARTER PEWTERSCHMIDT

Had Lois been born a boy, she would have been the perfect child.

Had Lois been born a boy, she would have been the perfect child. She was always very strong-willed and highly intelligent, but that pesky vagina always got in the way of her ability to be truly great. Originally, we had high hopes for her older brother, Patrick, until he started murdering people. And not the good kind of covert C.I.A murder, but the sloppy, angry, *America's Most Wanted*, lower-class type of murder. Once I accepted the fact that the opening between Lois's legs was not going to heal, and that she would never be an American president, I began to look forward to a bright future for her as a senator. It wasn't until the fat man came into her life that all of my hopes for her were dashed. Peter Griffin was and is an obese black cloud that will forever darken my days.

A+

My Summer Vacation with Daddy and an Exploration of the Electra Complex

by Lois Pewterschmidt

A+

Winning in Vietnam and Other Fairy Tales

by Lois Pewterschmidt

A+

Is Pacman a Racist Game, Pitting the Yellow Man Against Us All?

by Lois Pewterschmidt

Lois for Class President

We Regret to Announce

The Engagement of Our Daughter,

Lois Anabelle Pewterschmidt

to

Steaming-Pile-of-Shit Griffin

VOTE FOR LOIS!
Being popular and being a good, fair leader don't always go hand-in-hand.

WHITE SKIN GOOD. BROWN SKIN ALSO OKAY.

Chapter 2
Political Afterbirth

I got my first taste of public office in high school. I ran for class president in my senior year and won! To be honest, it was hardly a landslide victory. **I held the very unpopular position that the cafeteria workers and janitors at our private school were, in fact, people.** My platform was one of equality as reflected in my motto, "White skin good. Brown skin also okay. Vote for Lois!" It was a very close race, and I later learned that I might not have won if it weren't for my third period History teacher, whom I had been sleeping with ever since my eighteenth birthday. I guess he promised people extra credit if they voted for me. (*sigh*) Oh, Mr. Tuffy . . . he always smelled like cigars and whiskey.

As we have seen with President Bush, it doesn't matter how a person gets into office, it is what he or she does when they are there that matters. Once serving as President of Newport Academy, I immediately changed school policy, making it NO LONGER OKAY to toss your lunch leftovers in the cafeteria workers' faces. It was NO LONGER OKAY to dissect retired janitors either. And most importantly, it was NO LONGER OKAY to impregnate Sharon Hendricks and then just throw money at her under the bleachers. As you can imagine, I wasn't exactly the most loved president that served in the annals of Newport Academy's history… (*Ha! I typed "annals" and they printed it!*) But being popular and being a good, fair leader don't always go hand-in-hand. This was an important lesson I carried with me into my future careers, both as a mother and as Mayor of Quahog.

A Word from
BABS PEWTERSCHMIDT

When Lois was born I was so happy and relieved that she wasn't deformed. I smoked Carlton 100's all through my pregnancy with an occasional vodka gimlet to wash away the lower back pain, so I wasn't sure what to expect when she came out. She was simply adorable and such an easy baby, too. At least that's what Mimi told me. I enjoyed being a mother for many reasons, but mostly because it was like having a doll that you could dress up in pretty outfits and show off at the club!

My sweet Lois was a failed miscarriage.

My nanny Mimi was my everything and I was her favorite l'il cracker.

Chapter 3
Become the Man You Want to Elect

I believe that any reasonable, thinking person would have made the decision to run for office had they been in my shoes standing before Mayor Adam West that fateful day. Peter, the kids, and I were taking a family vacation at Lake Quahog when we discovered that the lake had been contaminated by waste. The spill-off coming from big business had been sanctioned, unbeknownst to me and most of Quahog's residents, by our own mayor, Mr. Adam West. We were victims—all of us. Our own government was running away with our rights. Our right to a healthy environment. Our right to full disclosure concerning our own safety. And our right to representation free of collusion.

Beware of TOXINS!

I had known Mayor West for many years before our competition at the polls. I had, in fact, voted for him in the last election. And truth be told, **I was a huge *Batman* fan! I loved watching him jump around in those tights. And he never seemed to get chaffed.** (There must have been a lot of ball powder on that set!) It was just so exciting to see him get behind the wheel of that dark mysterious car en route to kicking some serious ass. So, imagine my surprise and disappointment to find myself running against the very man I had held in such high regard for so many years. But I felt it was my civic duty to put an end to his corruption and to give the people of Quahog the fair and honest leadership they so rightly deserved.

A Word from
MAYOR ADAM WEST

> Twizzlers make mouths happy.

Hello, Reader. When I heard that Lois Griffin was going to be running for mayor of Quahog against me, my first thought was, "If a tree falls in the forest and I'm there to hear it, but it falls on my head, will my broken skull make a noise?" Then, when I heard she was going to be writing a book about her time in office, I thought to myself, **"Twizzlers make mouths happy."** **(Or if your mouth is clinically depressed, stable.)**

Then, when she asked me to contribute a chapter to her book, I decided that I better learn how to read and write, because I don't draw very well.

Reader, I always knew that I would be Mayor of Quahog, just as I always knew that the sky is blue, that the plural of moose is meese, and that "Player's Holiday" is the best song ever written. I was born to lead. But there are other things in life besides running a town, things that I didn't have time to partake in until ~~Die Redhead Die~~ Lois Gri— Gro—her last name escapes me right now—took over the position of mayor, giving me my first real vacation in years. I used this time very wisely, engaging in many recreational activities, as well as checking off a few things on my grand life's to-do list. Below is a small window into what I accomplished during Lois's time in office:

1. Read all of the Babysitters' Club books while continuing to ignore the Sweet Valley High books.

2. Went to Vegas for a quickie marriage. To whom? Wouldn't you like to know. And wouldn't I.

3. Became very good at ultimate Frisbee.

4. Became even better at non-ultimate Frisbee.

5. Finally found time to write that fan letter to my favorite cereal.

Dear Cookie Crisp,
I think you would win in a fight against Oreos because even though you are smaller, there are more of you in one box. Safety in numbers.

Yours, etc. Adam West

6. Spent more time with my pet falcon, Steven.

7. Dabbled in photography. You can see here an example of one of my photos, which I developed by hand in my very own darkroom. I'm scared of the dark, so I had a lamp on in there.

Here's one of Steven that didn't turn out quite as well: ⟶

8. Spirograph!

Too bad for my life's to-do list, but good for Quahog, Lois Griffin's reign as mayor was short-lived. Obviously, she did not have the love for the city that I do, and to lead this city you have to love it. Here are some of the things I love* best about Quahog:

THE "ADAM WEST" SANDWICH at Cleveland's Deli, a delightful mixture of corned beef, Nutella, and my fingerprints. It takes a lot of time to run over and touch each sandwich when somebody orders one, but it's worth it. Your tastebuds will agree. I know mine do, except for the time I petted a stray dog on my way in.

JAMES WOODS. The mayorship is a stressful job, but the forest is a peaceful place, where I can get my best thinking done, as well as my best macramé. Here's a poncho I macraméd for my grandfather.

MEG GRIFFIN. **Did I hit that when she was an intern at my office? Yes, yes I did.** Do you know which definition of the word "hit" I'm using? No, no you don't. Ha on you.

THE OLD ABANDONED TRAIN TRACKS. It's great that they're abandoned because then when you put a penny on the tracks to flatten them, there is (their is? thare is?) very little chance you'll get hit by a—OH MY GOD, THERE IS A STAR OUTSIDE IN THE SKY THAT IS WINKING AT ME. THAT IS SO INAPPROPRIATE, HOW DARE THAT STAR. I'VE HALF A MIND TO GO AND—

Here is my grocery list:

Stove Top stuffing
bananas
tin foil
Ecto cooler
milk — it does a body good
orange juice — because
orange juice spokesman
from commercial is
handsome yet relatable
scotch tape
welsh tape
tapeworm
fresh flowers — for soup
garnish and other uses
Hi Adam, how are you enjoying
reading your list so far?
Adam, you have the best
handwriting did you ever
consider changing your
name to Floyd?
soup

* Love does not necessarily include monogamy. Sometimes I drive over to the lovely town of Smithfield. Woonsocket ain't bad either.

Reader, I know what you're thinking: how could an obviously insane man ever be elected mayor? And to that, I say: it is very rude to question Kwame Kilpatrick like that. He's done a lot for Detroit. As for Quahog, I would like to share with you what would happen in the event that I am ever shot, decapitated, pulverized, liquefied, drawn and quartered, electrocuted, eaten by piranhas, beaten with live chinchillas, or otherwise killed and/or rendered unable to continue in office. Please see the below flow chart for who would succeed me:

MAYORAL SUCCESSION FLOW CHART

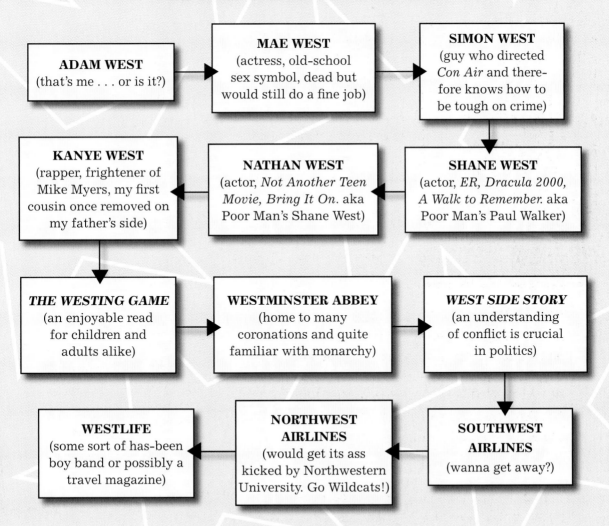

ADAM WEST
(that's me . . . or is it?)

MAE WEST
(actress, old-school sex symbol, dead but would still do a fine job)

SIMON WEST
(guy who directed *Con Air* and therefore knows how to be tough on crime)

KANYE WEST
(rapper, frightener of Mike Myers, my first cousin once removed on my father's side)

NATHAN WEST
(actor, *Not Another Teen Movie, Bring It On*. aka Poor Man's Shane West)

SHANE WEST
(actor, *ER, Dracula 2000, A Walk to Remember*. aka Poor Man's Paul Walker)

THE WESTING GAME
(an enjoyable read for children and adults alike)

WESTMINSTER ABBEY
(home to many coronations and quite familiar with monarchy)

WEST SIDE STORY
(an understanding of conflict is crucial in politics)

WESTLIFE
(some sort of has-been boy band or possibly a travel magazine)

NORTHWEST AIRLINES
(would get its ass kicked by Northwestern University. Go Wildcats!)

SOUTHWEST AIRLINES
(wanna get away?)

Last, but not least, and possibly most, here is a recipe for what I love more than my job.

MAYOR WEST'S TAFFY RECIPE

This recipe has been in my family for generations. It was created by my great-great-grandmother Mrs. Wilhemina "Snake Eyes" West. Over the years, it has been tweaked, improved, and occasionally worsened. There have also been other things done to it, but I can't go into that here. Shhhhh.

For delicious taffy you will need:

2 cups sugar

1 cup light corn syrup

1 cup water

1/2 or 1 or 1 1/2 teaspoon salt (depending on your taste preference and blood pressure)

2 tablespoons butter (Do not use margarine. I have no idea what will happen if you do, and cannot be held responsible if it turns out unpleasantly. Also, do not use Crisco. Or baby oil. Or sunscreen.)

1 teaspoon vanilla extract (You can also use peppermint or some other flavorful extract OR no flavoring if you are not feeling very flavorful.)

Food coloring. I won't tell you how much because I don't want to stifle your creativity. This world is all about choices. You might make the choice not to add any food coloring at all. Aha! Brave choice, soldier. Sail on.

1. Combine sugar, corn syrup, water, and salt in a pot. Over low heat, stir until sugar dissolves, then gently boil without stirring until a candy thermometer reads about 260° and

a bit of the mixture dropped into cold water forms a ball that is firm enough to hold its shape.

2. Remove from heat and stir in butter until melted. Add vanilla extract or other flavoring, and food coloring if you so desire. For a joke you might use peppermint extract, but then yellow food coloring, creating a minty candy that looks like a lemony candy. Think of the confused look on people's faces! Ha! Ha! What will they do now that their taste buds are telling them something different than their eyeballs? Who knows! Their heads might even explode!

3. Pour mixture into a buttered cake pan. Oh, darn it, you probably need more butter then, to butter the pan. I should have told you to get more butter before. I apologize. You also need a cake pan. I apologize for not previously mentioning the cake pan as well. Let mixture sit in the pan until it has cooled down enough to handle. Butter your hands—oh no, now you need even more butter. I am so, so sorry. Please return to the beginning of this recipe and where it says—2 tablespoons butter—pretend it says a lot more butter than that. Thank you. Now with your buttered hands, start pulling the bejeezus out of the taffy. This will take a while. You will know when the bejeezus has been successfully pulled out because it will be satiny-looking and light in color. Pull into ropes, cut into 1-inch pieces, wrap the pieces in waxed paper, and twist the ends of the waxed paper. Oh no. I should have told you to get some waxed paper, too. I apologize again.

Then enjoy! And make sure to feed some to your pet falcon. They get angry when they're hungry.

IT'S TRUE. WE DO!

Chapter 4
Running with Breasts Requires More Support

My campaign was not an easy one. The odds were stacked against me both as a woman, and as a first-time candidate. I knew that I had to prove to the people of Quahog that my will was strong and that my politics always leaned toward the needs of the masses, but what could I do about the fact that I was born a woman? How could I convince a community that had never before put its faith in a female leader that it was okay to do so? That I could be trusted? That I wouldn't ruin our fair city just because my penis is on the inside? **What I needed was an image makeover.** So, I took a meeting with a Publicist/Image Expert. His name was Raul, and he is so on-fire gay that he almost swings all the way around again, coming off as homophobic and angry. That's right, Raul is an angry, effeminate, homophobic, gay Latino man and I love him! (He calls me his little "Empanada Roja!")

Raul and I spent the first day poring over dozens of before-and-after pictures of all the women in politics and media who preceded me. I've included some of them for you to enjoy.

Hillary Clinton Before

Hillary Clinton After

Barbara Boxer Before

Barbara Boxer After

Raul showed me how to dig deep inside to discover the many faces of me. **(He also showed me this incredible method of walking like I'm carrying a baby bird in my ass. "Tight, but delicate, my Empanada Roja!" he'd say.)** Here are some of the various "faces of Lois" that we discovered on the journey toward my campaign:

This was my "Black Panther, Angela mutha-fu#!&* Davis" look.

Oh, and here's my blind Annie look.

I was going for a Gwen Stefani thing but ended up with more of a Pippi Long-stocking or Wendy's look here.

This was my "one freckle for every guy I dated" look (à la Lindsay Lohan).

Ah, and who could forget my "run Lois, run" look.

After a lot of trial and error we finally settled on this:

Me. The real me. Raul showed me that the strongest weapon I had in my corner was the ease with which I related to every person in Quahog. I was one of them. I went to the same market, joined the same PTA, and drove in the same carpools. I did have to make one big change however: **Raul put me on a 3,000 calorie-a-day eating program to help make my thighs and ass a bit bigger.** This was done so that the women of Quahog wouldn't hate me. A woman will only vote for another woman if she believes the other woman to be fatter than she is.*

* *New England Journal of Medicine,* "Independent Study on Hateful Women Who Hate Women"; February 15, 2006.

A Word from RAUL the Publicist

When I first met Lois I knew that she had what it took to jump into the political arena. She was smart, tireless, and extremely personable. She also had a perfect ass and great tits. **And I say this because I am a straight man who likes women a great deal.** I think that gays are gay. Sometimes when I go out dancing at gay clubs I get so angry at all the gay men that want to dance with me. It's like, "Why are you looking at me?" You know? Sometimes the anger takes over and before I know it I am dancing with them and then kissing them passionately. Occasionally, my anger explodes all over the strong sweaty backs of one of the gays. Man, I feel sorry for them. The gays.

Uno Momento Con la Publicista RAUL

Cuando conocí Lois yo sabía que ella comprendía los jugetes políticos. Ella estaba intelligente, incansable, y era muy simpático. Tambien, ella tenía nalgas perfectas y tetas irresistables. ¡Digo eso porque soy un hombre macho y me gustan mucho las mujeres! **Pienso que los maricones son "gay."** A veces cuando salgo a bailar en los clubes maricones me enojo a todos los homosexuales que quieren bailar con migo. ¿¿¿Es como, "Porque me miras???" ¿¿¿Sabes??? El enojo me agarra y antes que yo se, estoy bailando con los pansies y bessando a ellos apasionadamente. De vez en cuando mi enojo explota por todas partes de la espalda sudada del uno de los "gays." Híjole, you tengo lástima a ellos los maricones.

The next step was the most important and enjoyable part of my campaign.
Getting out there in the community and
meeting the people I wanted to represent
was exhilarating. I went to grocery stores,
malls, car dealerships, and parks. It was
like a freakin' Tiffany tour! We had ban-
ners and T-shirts, and pins that we handed
out everywhere we went. That's where my
children, Chris and Meg, really came in
handy. They each brought so much of their
own personality to the campaign. Meg was already dabbling with poetry so I
asked her to write some slogans and press releases for me. And my son Chris is a
very talented artist, so he was in charge of the advertising campaign. Here are
some of the various looks and slogans that we used on the campaign trail.

This was one of Meg's
and it's my favorite:

Peter helped inspire this one:

I think Raul designed
this button:

Daddy had this poster printed in Brazil. That's where Republicans outsource their printing:

Here are some of the rejected designs and slogans:

Not sure who was responsible for this one.

PEWTERSCHMIDT HAPPENS!

VOTE FOR LOIS AND LET'S MILK THE SYSTEM

VOTE FOR LOIS AND VOTE FOR THE BREAST

VOTE FOR LOIS

UNLESS YOU'RE A QUEER.

NO, WAIT, EVEN IF YOU'RE A QUEER.

NO JEWS, THOUGH.

OKAY, JEWS.

This was one of Peter's.

A Word from
CHRIS

Mom said I could write whatever I wanted in this book.

DOODIE!

Ha ha ha! I wrote "doodie" and you just read it. You'd think the editor would've made me take that out, huh? I bet they don't even read the whole book. Watch this, "Hey, editor lady! One time, I peed on my rental horse so no one else would ride him." See? I told you she wasn't paying attention. She was probably too busy *being beautiful and smart and very good at her job.*

I think it's pretty cool that my mom was the mayor of our town. All my friends thought it was way cool, too, but they always kinda liked my mom before. They'd say things like, "You can't spell Mrs. Lois Griffin without the letters M.I.L.F." And they'd say, "Your mom's cool 'cause she buys Sunny-D." (I guess that stuff's just too loaded with sugar for most moms to buy. Is it any wonder I'm so grotesquely overweight?)

Smell my finger.

Anyway, my favorite parts in all the books I own are the activities pages, so I thought I'd make some cool, fun games and stuff to give you something to do while you're on the bus, or waiting to go into the principal's office 'cause you trapped your fart in a cup during recess and then set it free in your music class. [Answers on page 87]

ANAGRAMS

An anagram is where you take the letters of one word or name and mix 'em up to make other words. For instance, an anagram for "Quahog Rhode Island" is **"Squalid, honored hag."** And an anagram for "Christopher Griffin" is **"I, French Frog, Rip Shit."** Ha ha ha! It's fun and there's usually more than one anagram for any word or name. See what you can come up with for Lois Griffin. How about Lois Pewterschmidt Griffin?

_____ _____

_____ _____

_____ _____

_____ _____

CONNECT THE DOTS

When you connect all the dots, you'll see what Meg sees after "seven minutes in heaven."

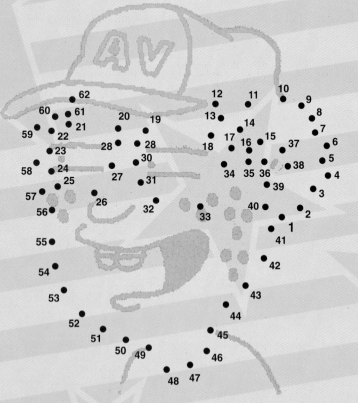

CROSSWORD PUZZLE

ACROSS

1   My middle name.
4   Word means penis, or
    to tire out, or Dad.
5   Always wants to give me
    candy and ambien.
8   The lady I came out of.
10 Word for bread or poop.
13 "Love is a ___.
14 God spelled backwards.
16 Runny bottom.

DOWN

2   Fancy word for fat.
3   Butt sneezes.
5   My favorite food.
6   Who lives in my closet?
7   Stewie's middle name.
9   What I make art with and
    also masturbate with.
11 Apple pie spice or my
    crazy sister.
12 Philosopher who claimed
    "God is dead."
15 What Raul is not?
17 Donkey.

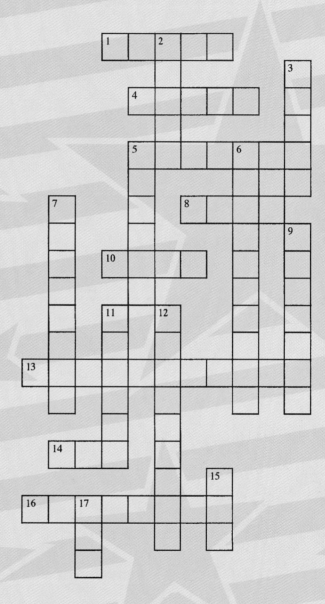

Here is some art I made!

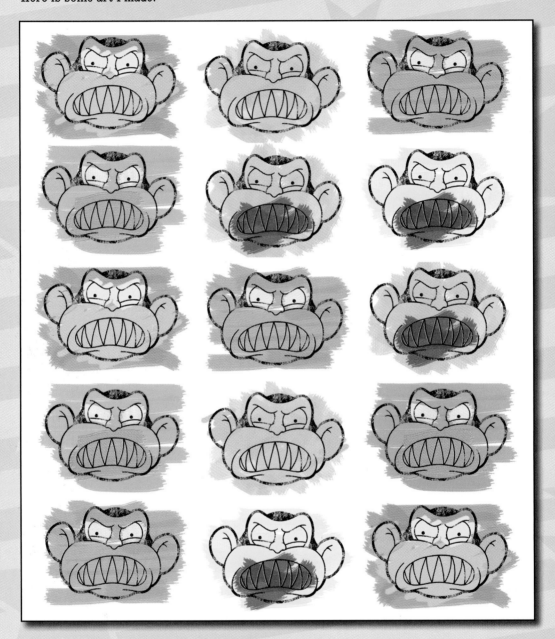

Christopher Cross Griffin, *Evil Monkey*, 2006.

A WORD FROM MEG

The unvarnished truth is that my mother has been making my life miserable for years.

So today Mom asked me to help her write a book. At first I totally thought, "Awesome! I'm gonna be a famous author, just like Jane Austen and Emily Brontë!"* Then she told me that the book was about her campaign for mayor and that whatever I wrote would have to be about how great a mother and leader and person she is, and **I realized that once again, she was gonna try and make everything all about her,** just like every boy who sees us together thinks she's so much hotter than me, just like anyone who talks to both of us thinks she's so much smarter than me, just like she's the one in the family who gets all the love and all the attention and I get nothing, **NOTHING**, even though she's my **MOTHER** and she's supposed to love and protect **ME** and all she does is steal the spotlight for herself, every time, **EVERY SINGLE TIME, THAT SKANKY SELF-CENTERED REDHEADED BITCH! Aaaaaaaaaaaahhhhhh!**

Anyway.

The unvarnished truth is that my mother has been making my life miserable for years. I mean, even as a toddler I knew that she was prettier than me—people were always telling her, "You look so great! You look so beautiful!" Then they'd look at me and say, "Oh, did you guys get another dog?" Let me tell you, comments like that do not do wonders for a child's self-esteem.† Especially when your mom cheerfully answers,

---

* Because nothing is cooler than being a lifelong spinster or dying of tuberculosis at age thirty. See "Famous Womyn Authors Who Filled Their Lives with Words Not Penis," by Tallulah Hyman.

† See "Why Don't I Look More Like Mom?" by Alexa Joel and Rumer Willis.

"Yes, a bulldog!" while scruffing your cheek jowls and pinching your rolls of stomach fat.

As I grew older it got even worse. It became clearer to me with each passing day how inferior I was to Mom, mostly because she kept telling me.

"Meg, you're *so* lucky you didn't have to wear a bra until you were sixteen! I had to start in the fifth grade and believe me, it was *very* distracting to have boys staring at me all the time during recess."

"Meg, that tan looks great on you! You should definitely go out in the sun more—the color does a wonderful job hiding your acne scars."

"Meg, you're fat and ugly. Just kidding—all of God's children are beautiful. Just not all of my children. Just kidding. Not really."

This doesn't even count the times I was about to get some action (thank heaven for chubby-chasers) and she'd suddenly walk in and bend over to "accidentally" show some cleavage, or casually brush past the guy while pretending to be reaching for the laundry basket. This would always lead the guy to a) forget I ever existed despite the fact that I was sitting right there and/or b) run to the bathroom, slam the door, and stay there for anywhere from several minutes to an hour, depending on whether my mom was hang-drying her handwashed lingerie in there.

So you can see, there are plenty of reasons why I might not want to help out my mom with her book.

But let's face it: it's not like I have anything better to do.

Also, I had a lot of alone time when Mom was campaigning. (Even more than normal. Brian locked me in the basement so that nobody would see my face and therefore vote for Mayor West instead of Mom. None of the family wanted to come and visit me, and if they had to get something out of the extra fridge they either waited till I was asleep or threw a baseball at my head on their way down the stairs in order to knock me out.) I spent those weeks thinking and writing about important issues that face teenage girls today. After all, if Jewel and Amber Tamblyn could write poetry and get it published—even though some people think they should've just stuck to their day jobs—why shouldn't I? So now, I would like to present to you my collected poetic endeavors from that time of solitude and reflection. I hope they will hold as much meaning for you as they do for me.

Are You There, God? It's Me, Meg

The Poetry and Photography of Megan "Fragile Bird"* Griffin

* I chose this name in defiance of the name my parents gave me. Frightened Child, Playful Dolphin, and
Shaves with Four Blades were also on the list, but ultimately the one I chose was the most accurate
representation of what I feel is my true self, along with being the least retarded.

The Changeling

In shorts too short
    For none to see
I stand behind the
    Metal door
Perhaps my pants
    Will cover these
And I won't have to
    Change once more
With the rancid odor
    Of P.E.
Between my legs as
    I watch the clock
Why the other girls can
    Shower free

From ridicule and
    Vicious mock
Ery will always be
    A mystery.
To me. To me. To me. P.E.

Birth Day

from betwixt her thighs
came a fount of pain
and the pain was me
and the pain is I
pain
pain
rain
pain
mama

Haiku

A shield for my brain.
Against the cold and the rain.
My pink condom hat.

One Headlight
aka Requiem For My Inverted Left Nipple

Please come out of hiding
     Befriend again your twin
          Reach out and touch her
               Find the beauty within

               For once you were so perky
          And now you are gone
     And now I am uneven
Because you are withdrawn

The Boys

The boys, they do
Not look at me
For I do not
Have double D's
And so I wait
With pained unease
In search of boys
To take pity

On me

The boys, they do
Not want to kiss
A girl whose looks
Are so remiss
And so my life
Has known no bliss
A boy is still
On my wish list

I'm pissed

The boys, they want
What I am not
They want a girl
Who's smoking hot
And so I sit
And so I rot
Oh what to do
With my life's lot?

~~Smoke pot~~
~~Get shot~~
~~Cry like a bitch~~
Finish this poem later after
watching *My Super Sweet 16*

Love Song for Craig Hoffman

He plays by no rules but his own
Sometimes
Not even his own
Brown of hair and blue of eye
Only he completes me
Only he can compete
No other boys can
No other soul
Oh Craig
Dear Craig
Make a woman of me
Or at least be near
Me
Feel my gaze
Acknowledge my tender touch
Upon your leather jacket arm
You've charmed
This girl
With relatively little effort
With a really rather miniscule quantity of effort
Seriously it didn't take much

Soliloquy

To douche or not to douche
That is the question

i saw red

the scarlet smear
upon the vine
oh how i wish i hadn't gotten my period while climbing the rope in gym class

Cave of Mystery

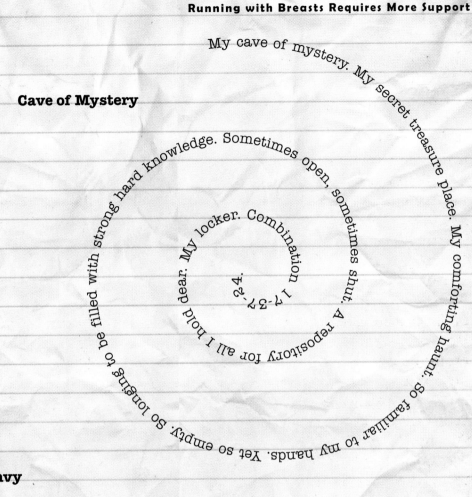

My cave of mystery. My secret treasure place. My comforting haunt. So familiar to my hands. Yet so empty. So longing to be filled with strong hard knowledge. Sometimes open, sometimes shut. A repository for all I hold dear. My locker. Combination 17-37-24.

Tit Envy

The bountiful curves that will never be mine
The velvety spheres I so wistfully regard
I survey my own chest and wait for a sign
That flesh will soon swell to help fill my dance card
But until that day
And until that hour
My life remains flat
My soul remains sour
Why?
Why?
Why can't I have breasts like my father?

Chapter 5
It Takes a Village Idiot

In the introduction to this book I talked about how I never would have made it to the Mayor's Office without the help of my family and friends. I know how cliché that sounds, but you must understand that it is one hundred percent accurate and true in this instance. It wasn't just the support and kind words of those around me that kept me going; it was their actions. Some were more hands-on than others, but they all helped me get the votes I needed to win. **So, I say thank you to each and every person who helped put me in office.** Thank you Peter, thank you Meg, thank you Chris, thank you Stewie, thank you Brian. And to the rest of my family, friends, and everyone else in the community, I say thank you, too. (And in the words of Alanis Morissette: "Thank you India, thank you terror, thank you disillusionment, thank you frailty, thank you consequence, thank you, thank you silence. And a very special thanks to Dave Coulier for making me so f&#king angry.")

A WORD FROM
QUAGMIRE

Lois. (*sigh*) Oh Lois. My sweet, sweet Lois. They say that to covet another man's wife is a sin. I bet that commandment was written by a guy with a big, tubby, dog of a woman for a wife. I bet she has fat rashes and her butt smells like Parmesan. You see, it's my belief that a woman who is coveted is worth coveting, and Lois Griffin fits the bill. I've said it before and I'll say it again: **I would give it all up for Lois. All of it!** The late nights, the layovers, the lay-unders (Giggety!), the beautiful women, the semi-hard inducing women . . . all of it. (The great thing about saying this is that I know Lois will never leave Peter, and Peter will never leave Lois, so I'll never have to walk the talk. (Wink. Wink.) But let me get to the point (Of my penis! Oh!) When I saw the mudslinging ads that were being launched against my Lois, I was ~~horny~~ sick, absolutely sick to my stomach. Like when I heard this ad on the radio:

ANNOUNCER: Every month a woman gets her period. Nine times out of ten, she'll become a temperamental bitch. Is that really what you want in a mayor? The highest ranking official in the city must be someone we can trust. Someone who will not be compromised by anything, including her own *hormones*. Someone who will never have to wrap a sweatshirt around her waist "just in case." Lois Griffin is bad for Quahog and a bad person in general. (*Beat, then*) Paid for by the American Association of Families Against Life Choices for People with Families Who Came from Families.

I was so shaken by this ad and others like it that right then and there, I committed myself to do whatever it took to insert Lois into office. (Just wanted to use the word "insert." Allllriiiight!) I immediately launched my own grassroots operation, which I called "Pimp the Vote!" With an '87 tour bus that I borrowed from my old pal Kenny Loggins (we used to do shots and play cards back in Everett, Washington, until he got that weird haircut and wrote "This Is It" and

wouldn't take it back), I drove into the darkest corners of Quahog. **It was late and I was tired, but I knew one thing—Lois needed me—and that was motivation enough.** I pulled up to a familiar spot under a streetlamp where several leggy ladies milled about, dressed in faux fur and gold lamé. The bus hissed as the door seductively opened.

"Hey Q-man," said one of the women, dressed in pink.

"Evenin', Pinky," I replied. "Say, any of you gals got social security numbers?"

"Come on man, you know we get tested," barked Pinky.

At that point I knew I had to lay it on the line . . . for Lois.

I said, "Girls, I need a huge favor and you're just gonna have to get on this bus and trust me."

At that moment, several of the windows on the vehicle slid open, revealing the many other "ladies of the night" that had gotten on board earlier in the evening. From my side-view mirror I could see Sandra lean out and call, "Hey Pinky! Come on and get yourself on this here hooker bus! We're gonna get registered and vote. Glen says it'll be empowering and a nice break for our labias."

Pinky thought for a moment then said, "Labium."

"What?" Sandra asked.

"The plural of labia is labium," stated Pinky as she bent over to fluff her hooters.

Sandra took this new information in as if it were her very first breath. "Oh," she said.

These women never cease to amaze me. They are at once so very shallow and so very deep (some deeper than others. Oh!)

"So how 'bout it, ladies?" I asked.

Pinky tossed her boa up and around her neck and enthusiastically hopped on the bus. **(It was pretty cool to watch her ta-tas bounce!)** All of the other ladies followed suit and climbed on board my huge, long, hard bus, saying things like, "Sounds fun," "I'm up for anything," and "I'm not sure I can sit down, but I'm game!"

I closed the bus doors and slowly pulled away, knowing right then that I would never have Lois—or any one woman—because these girls needed me.

Everything in the world was just as it should be, and I was going to deliver the precious votes that would help Lois win.

On a side note, here is a list of other favorite female politicians and what I'd like to do to them:

MADELINE ALBRIGHT
(The 64th U.S. Secretary of State)
"I'd take her doggystyle. Wouldn't wanna see what was comin', but how can I resist? She's one of the greatest thinkers of our time and can talk dirty in seven different languages. Note: A sturdy old gal might be able to lift me."

HILLARY CLINTON
(First Lady of Arkansas, First Lady of the United States, Senator from New York)
"I'd do it all to her. If you give it a little squint, this one holds up."

SANDRA DAY O'CONNOR
(First female Justice of the United States Supreme Court)
"I'd make out with Sandy hard and slow, never opening my eyes. I'd have her keep her robe on while I find my way around down there. So supreme!"

BARBARA BOXER
(United States Senator from California)
"I bet this one's wild. Most Jewish chicks really know how to let go. They're all bossy and controlling by day, but at night they just want someone else to take over. Isn't that right, Barbara? Maybe a little reverse cowgirl? How 'bout a stand-y in the shower? Call me."

CONDOLEEZZA RICE
(National Security Advisor, The 66th and current U.S. Secretary of State)
"I'm on top with this one. But first, dinner, dancing and some delicious wine. We talk about foreign policy and how we both studied international politics under Josef Korbel, who happens to be the father of Madeline Albright. Small world, isn't it? Small, and funny . . . and fine. Man, I'd love to tongue that tooth gap!"

CHELSEA CLINTON
(Daughter of William Jefferson Clinton, the 42nd U.S. President)
"I have always found Chelsea to be a beautiful girl. I never paid any mind to what fools said about her, their disparaging remarks. She is, and always has been smokin' hot! Those big supple lips, that gorgeous mane of hair, her six-figure salary. This chick is perfect. With Chelsea I would do nothing but learn from her. Follow her lead. I am hopeful it'll take me to the White House where I can serve as her First Gentleman and re-do the Oval Office. I ♥ U Chelsea!"

Well, my time is up, but before I go, I want to leave you, the reader, my friend, with this very precious gift. This incredible centerfold of Lois Griffin, that I keep in my wallet, is yours to enjoy as I have for quite some time. (As you can see. Giggety goo!)

A Word from CLEVELAND

Hi, I'm Cleveland Brown. You know, when Peter came to me and asked if I'd help Lois get elected I said, **"You bet your big honky ass I will!"** And here's why: do y'all remember when the levees broke here in Quahog, and all the black people in town were over at my house?

We were stuck on that roof for days. Mayor West was slow to respond and do you know why? **Because Mayor West doesn't care about black people.** There, I said it.

So that's why I chose to support Lois Pewterschmidt Griffin. She loves black people (especially the men). I was out

DON'T TRUST WHITEY!
(BUT LOIS AIN'T THAT BAD AS FAR AS WHITEYS GO.)

there every day of the campaign, handing out T-shirts and bumper stickers with Ollie Williams, to show my support.

Ollie and I were instrumental in getting the black vote for Lois, so imagine our surprise when we showed up to the polls only to be turned away. The lines were around the corner and it, inexplicably, began to rain. After waiting for over an hour, Ollie and I finally made our way into the gymnasium at James Woods High. The poll-worker ran her old, boney, retired finger down the list and said that both my name and Ollie's were not there. I said, "Excuse me, but I have lived at the same house on Spooner Street for over five years now and I have always voted at this polling place." They checked the list again, but my name was nowhere to be found. Even Ollie, whose face was on the TV every night in Quahog, was not on the list. To which Ollie responded, "This is bullshit!" We had no alternative but to ask for provisional ballots and hope that our votes would, eventually, be counted.

When the final votes were tallied and Lois was elected Mayor of Quahog, I felt such a sense of pride to finally have a sister in office. **On the outside, Lois may not appear to be black, but on the inside, she is a rare Nubian princess.** In fact, one of the very first things she did as Mayor of Quahog was to swap out the white Jesus with a black Jesus in the nativity scene at the Quahog Mall. She also made changes to the aptitude tests at the public schools to include vocabulary words like "dimpled chads" and the new Three R's: "recovery," "reclamation," and "restoration." We still have a long way to go toward racial equality in this world, but people like Lois are getting us closer every day. (Please note: Lois also has quite a bit of junk in her trunk, which I find nice to look at when she walks.)

Lois loves black people (especially the men).

44

A Word from JOE

I'm not a man of many words, so I'll keep my comments brief, and to the point. (Like my penis. Kidding! My penis is huge, but dead.) I knew that if Lois Griffin was going to win that election, she would need the endorsement of the Quahog Police Department. I also knew that getting her that endorsement wouldn't be easy. It was very busy at the precinct that week, what with the new Fetus Fingerprinting program in full swing. (The idea is to get fingerprints as soon as possible to help curb any in utero crime from being committed within the last trimester.) The installation of the program meant that we would have a full house of officers there for training, so I jumped at the opportunity to give a little speech.

"Hi crime stoppers!" I said. To which they responded, "Hi Joe!" (This was good—I had them eating out of my hands, which were filthy from handling the wheels on my wheelchair all day. It's pretty unsanitary if you think about it. I mean, the wheels roll through mud and spit and shit all day.) I continued my speech, "Right now due to budget cuts, Mayor West only provides each of us with three bullets for our guns. Now, our guns hold six bullets, people. **That's fifty percent of our firepower gone!** That means we can only shoot half the people we wanna shoot! And that, my friends, is a bunch of crap if I've ever heard any!"

There were grumblings and I could tell that I'd really hit a nerve (like I did when I fell off the roof and became paralyzed that one Christmas, so long ago). I continued, "Now, if you vote for Lois Griffin on Tuesday, she promises to get every Quahog police officer five bullets each. Do the math people! Five is more than three. That's five dead suspects. That's five mortally wounded kids that you thought were holding guns that were really iPods. That's five shots into the sky if you're Mexican and it's New Year's Eve! Five *is* more than three!"

Quahog Times

LOIS PEWTERSCHMIDT GRIFFIN GETS POLICE ENDORSEMENT BECAUSE FIVE IS MORE THAN THREE

INFAMOUS FETUS BANDIT FINALLY APPREHENDED AND SHOT FIVE TIMES

A Word from HERBERT

Good evenin', good people. Well, I ain't never been asked to write a book before, lessen you count my slambook. Hey, maybe after you read this here book, you'd like to write a little somethin' in my slambook. You can find it at **www.herbertslambook.com.** It'll just take a few minutes and there's all kinds of fun questions for ya.

Here are some of the questions from my slambook with my answers:

In large print for older readers

Oh, this is really gonna chill your balls . . .

What's your favorite hair color? Blond.

What do you think is sexier, a walker or a cane?

A walker!

Do you prefer an HMO or a PPO? I don't have insurance right now.

Are you hot or not?

Hot, but then sometimes very cold for no reason.

What's your favorite prescription medication?
Ambien. And Ritalin.

Would you rather have your next birthday party at the Drunken Clam, the Fuzzy Clam, or somewhere else?
Chuck E. Cheese

What's your screensaver?
A rotation of personal photographs. *Personal.*

What's your favorite smell? Fixodent.

What's your least favorite smell? Women's perfume.

What are your top five books?

Oliver Twist by Charles Dickens

The Adventures of Tom Sawyer by Mark Twain

The Age of Innocence by Edith Wharton

Little Men by Louisa May Alcott

Bless the Beasts and Children by Glendon Swarthout

What is on your mousepad? Denture cream and sperm.

Have you ever been in love? Hell yes!

But I digress. I should be a gracious guest and write a little somethin' 'bout Lois Griffin's time in office like I said I would. Here goes . . .

To be honest, I enjoyed having Lois and her family suddenly thrown into the spotlight because it meant a million photographs of my precious Chris would be published in the *Daily Shopper*. I clipped out every photo that they printed and taped them to the wall in my bedroom until the powder blue wallpaper was completely covered. I wrote a few letters to Chris, and even talked to him on the phone a couple times, but I just couldn't get his attention. The attention that I felt I rightly deserved, goddammit. I finally decided that I had to do somethin' drastic. I had to make somethin' of myself, and quick. But how? **I decided that I would win Chris over by assassinatin' the mayor of Quahog.** It would make me a historical figure and therefore Chris's equal. It worked for John Hinckley Jr. Say, did you know that his father, John Hinckley Sr., was a huge oil man in Texas? Hinckley Oil was the name of his company, and he was a big-time contributor to George H. W. Bush's 1980 presidential primary campaign *against* Ronald Reagan. Well, ole John Hinckley Sr.'s energy company, Vanderbilt Energy, was being audited by the U.S. Department of Energy at that time. In fact, on the morning of March 30th, the federal government was threatening Hinckley's company with a $2 million fine. That same morning, an attempt was made on President Reagan's life by none other than John Hinckley Jr. himself. **I ask you, is that some kind of a coinky-dink, or what?** Now get ready for this: oh, this is really gonna chill your balls. . . . Hinckley Jr. had a brother, Scott, who, the very next day, had dinner plans with Neil Bush, our current president's brother. Mmmmmmm. I don't wanna use the "c" word, but somethin's fishy, for sure.*

As you can imagine, havin' all this information about Hinckley swirling around in my head made my woody turn to sawdust. It also made

---

* *The Houston Post*, March 31, 1981. This was widely reported by the AP, UPI, NBC News and *Newsweek*.

me come to my senses. I realized that if Chris was ever gonna love me, it would have to be for *me*. Not for some crazy scheme or because I killed his mama, but for me, Herbert. I'm a good man, people. I got myself a good heart and a kind soul and it may take a few years, but I think Chris will see that one day. And frankly, that fat little morsel is well worth the wait.

A Word from SEAMUS

When Lois be campaignin', I composed her this political version of a classic sea shanty. If ye want to sing it properly, take a shot of rum in between every line and see if ye make it to the end. I know I never have.

"CRAZY MAYOR"
(to the tune of "Drunken Sailor")

What shall we do with a crazy mayor?
What shall we do with a crazy mayor?
What shall we do with a crazy mayor?
Run a lass against him.

Way up the polls she rises.
Quahog's gonna see a few surprises.
Doesn't matter what between her thighs is.
Women can be leaders.

Believe the sassy redhead.
She'll improve the town and crime will be dead.
Plus her husband says she's freaky in bed.
Vote for Lois Griffin!

49

A Word from
TOM TUCKER and DIANE SIMMONS

As reporters, we are held to the highest standards of truth-telling. On our nightly newscasts, we always report the facts exactly as they happened, with absolutely zero embellishment. And we certainly never offer our own opinion—HAHAHAHAHAHA my God, even we can't keep straight faces when saying that. **Come on. As if reporters and "news" programs aren't just the same old trashy entertainment-based television you see on every other channel.** Please. So why sugarcoat it? Here is a chart of our unvarnished opinion on various aspects of Lois Griffin and her campaign to become mayor—does she have mad game or is she so lame? You decide. Just kidding—we already decided for you.

COVERING QUAHOG LIKE A WET BLANKET!

· TRICIA TAKANAWA · TOM TUCKER · DIANE SIMMONS ·

DIANE SIMMONS

TOM TUCKER

ON LOIS GRIFFIN'S . . .

Haircut

Mad game. It looks great on her, yet conveys a sense of professionalism. A practical, easy-to-care-for style for an intelligent, on-the-go woman.

So lame. If we wanted to look at a red-headed Bruce Jenner, that guy would still have a career instead of having to rely on crap reality-show paychecks to finance his scarily bad plastic surgery.

Voice

So lame. That nasal sound is hardly one you want to hear for forty-five minutes at a time during the "State of the City" address.

Mad game. I don't know who writes her speeches, but somehow she can make even the word "constituency" sound sexy. Or maybe that's just because it contains the word "tit."

Family

Mad game. The fact that Lois can run a household, raise children, and govern a town all at the same time just proves that women really can do it all.

Mad game. Why? Because chicks in aprons are hot. Especially if that's all they're wearing, and if they're also smacking you around with a spatula.

Campaign Strategies

So lame. Lois pandered to the masses in order to secure the vote.

Mad game. It's sexily Machiavellian to tell people what they want to hear in order to get them to do whatever you tell them to.

That weird patch of scaly skin on Diane's left hip

Wait, what?

What? It's there. We both know it.

My incredibly sexy mustache

Tom, this is extremely inappropriate. Since when is this chart about you?

Since always, baby. You didn't mind so much when Mr. Mustache was tickling you that night.

Diane's need for Botox

I'm sorry, but this is just getting ridiculous. These are personal matters between the two of us (that only happened once, by the way, and I cannot believe you chose this public forum to speak about it). Besides, I look great for my age.

Whatever you say, Grandma.

Chapter 6

Election Day

(or as Tricia Takanawa's mom would say, "Erection Day")

Election day was so exciting!

Only two other days in my life can match the excitement and anticipation I felt on that day: my wedding day, and the day I discovered being on top. Campaign headquarters (aka our house) was buzzing from the moment we all woke up. There were people crawling all over the place: volunteers, reporters, friends, family. **I think the only time we had any privacy was right after Peter used the downstairs bathroom and didn't turn on the fan.** (It was a real eggy stinker, too! The kind he usually saves up for a visit to my parents' house or when he knows Meg wants to take a bath.)

It was touch-and-go all day, with news reports first declaring me the winner, then Mayor West the winner, then me the winner. . . . It was nerve-wracking,

GRIFFIN PREDICTED TO
WIN BY CLOSE MARGIN

to say the least. The worst offender was Tom Brokaw on NBC, who at noon declared Mayor West the winner and then shot a confetti cannon all over the newsroom. He then changed into his sneakers and sweater, like Mr. Rogers, turned off the lights and left. All we saw on the air for the next few hours was a janitor sweeping up the confetti.

After night had fallen and the ballots were all counted (not including Cleveland or Ollie's, as theirs never made it into the ballot boxes), we all stood in the living room holding hands. Peter had to be on the end of the line because he wanted to have one hand down his pants as they read the official results. It's always been a dream of his. *Channel Five News*'s Asian correspondent Tricia Takanawa was with us at the house to get our live reaction on camera. It was actually Tricia who informed me that I was, in fact, the new Mayor of Quahog. I couldn't believe it! I think I screamed; I'm not sure. It was kind of like giving birth, where you're not quite certain if you're screaming or shitting on the delivery table. It was incredible! **I was so caught up in the moment I think I may have kissed Tricia.** Long and hard and on the lips. And I think she forced her tongue into my mouth. (Tricia is a very good kisser, and, FYI, her tongue is pierced. Writing about it now I still get chills. It is a day I will not soon forget.)

Here is a copy of my acceptance speech:*

"Oh my God. I'm sorry. This moment is so much bigger than me. This moment is for Dorothy Dandridge, Lena Horne, Diahann Carroll. It's for the women that stand beside me—Jada Pinkett, Angela Bassett and it's for every nameless, faceless woman of color that now has a chance because this door tonight has been opened.

Thank you. I'm so honored. I am so honored and thank the Academy for choosing me to be the vessel from which this blessing might flow. Thank you.

I want to thank my husband, Peter Griffin. He's been with me for many years and you've fought every fought [sic] and you've loved me when I've been up. But more importantly you've loved me when I've been down. You have been a lover, a friend, and the best father I've ever known, and I love you very much.

I want to thank my mom who's given me the strength to fight every single day to be who I want to be and given me the courage to dream that this dream might be happening and possible for me. I love you Mom so much.

* Some of this speech may have been inspired by the great Ms. Halle Berry.

page 2

Thank you to my kids who are just the joys of my life. And Brian— thank you for giving me peace because only with the peace that you've brought me have I been allowed to go to places that I never even knew I can go. Thank you, I love you and Brian with all my heart.

Thought you might get a kick out of the first version of the speech:

Fu*%!& yes! I Fu*%!& did it! I Fu*%& rule! And Adam West can kiss my black ass! Whoo!

A Word from
TRICIA TAKANAWA

When Mayor Griffin decided to give me a page in this book, I decided to do with it what I damn well please. Here are some groovy things about being Asian that have little or nothing to do with Lois.

I boned Yao Ming.

- If you live in a predominantly white city like Quahog, there's no competition for the A-cup bras at the store.

- Whenever you're feeling bad about the above, just remember: the bigger they are, the harder they fall.

- We look really young . . . at least until we're about 60, when we suddenly start looking 100.

- There are more of us than there are of you. I think. If not, there will be soon.

- Catholic schoolgirl outfits look extra skanky on us.

- When we breed with other races the results are hot, except for Rob Schneider.

- Who invented karaoke? That's right.

- Who did *not* invent AIDS? Exactly. (And don't you dare throw bird flu in my face, because bird flu is still just the Haylie Duff to AIDS's Hilary.)

- People think you're smart even if you're not. My IQ is 67, but that hasn't seemed to have damaged my reporting career any.

- Looking all the same means it's much easier to pin the crimes you commit on other people.

- Good things come in small packages.

- I boned Yao Ming. This is completely irrelevant—I just wanted to tell you.

A Word from
BRUCE, THE PERFORMANCE ARTIST

Hey there. How y'all doin'? Thanks for turning to this page. I appreciates it. I'm just gonna tell you how I helped out with Ms. Lois Griffin's mayoral campaign on election day. I worked them polls, you know, cheerin' up the registered voters as they waited in line, helpin' read instructions about how to pull them levers. Just keepin' people company, handin' out cupcakes with red, white, and blue frosting that I baked up the night before. It wasn't too hard . . . some cake mix, some different food colorings. Some sprinkles shaped like L's and G's. Everybody likes a treat. **Tell you a secret—in a couple of them cupcakes I baked a spoonful of strawberry jam right there in the middle, so some peoples got a little surprise. A little extra sweetness in their day.** Maybe get 'em thinking about other ways that foodstuffs can be used, maybe in some new and exciting ways. Maybe think about using food in a relaxing manner or whatnot, with yourself, with a loved one. But not in such a naughty way that you get arrested for public lewdness or give yourself a nasty infection. The kind of infection that necessitates a hospital visit and some prescription medication, and maybe the humiliation was worth the fun, but maybe not. But at least it's not a situation you've gotten yourself into any time recently. That's all in your past, mostly.

Vests keep all your vital organs all nice and cozy, while keepin' your pits fresh and dry. God bless vests.

Chapter 7
Mayor Griffin

My time in office can best be described as both my proudest achievement and my biggest failure. (I'm guessin' Elizabeth Berkley felt pretty much the same after *Showgirls* opened in theaters.) Prior to holding office, it was very easy for me to sit and judge Mayor West and his administration, but once I was perched behind the wheel of democracy, I saw for myself just how easily it could be steered right off the road.

I had Quahog's best interest at heart initially. My first plan of attack was aimed at cleaning up Lake Quahog. It had been so badly tainted by carcinogens, it was kinda like the womb of Tony Montoya's girlfriend in *Scarface*. **"Her womb is so polluted, I can't even have a fu#$!& little baby with her."** So, to clean up the lake, I proposed that we raise Quahog residents' property taxes just a little. Let me tell you—people nearly soiled themselves. And not a nice, neat, solid kind of soil, but a wet, sloppy, corn-filled kind of soil. You see, people are all talk. They say they want things like new roads, better schools, and cleaner environments, but when it comes down to incurring any costs they all change their tunes. No one is willing to sacrifice for the greater good. Shouldn't we strive for a community in which all of our children have access to a high-quality, free education? A community in which those same children also have health insurance? Don't get me wrong, I'm no communist with thoughts of abolishing capitalism for the common good. I'm more of an Eduard Bernstein fan than a Marxist. I believe that we can create true socialism through capitalism. We need the rich to get richer and pay more taxes to make these things, like better schools, possible. But here's the problem: what happens is that many rich people, like my parents, gradually want to pay fewer and fewer taxes. Money fosters God complexes and leaves the wealthy with a sense of entitlement and immunity. Immunity to the woes of the world. Immunity to the reality of daily life and the obstacles it holds for those of us without extra income. I know that it's not really both of my parents that are to blame—it's mostly Daddy and his conservative, small-thinking brain.

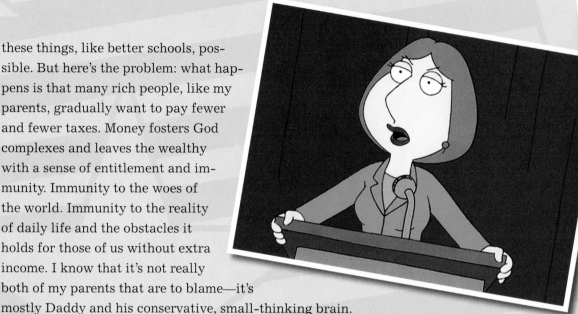

He was always so controlling growing up. I'm pretty sure that's what started my bout with bulimia. Well, that and my obsession with Cathy Rigby. Boy was she fat! But I digress . . .

    I soon found that I was twisting my own words around, telling the people of Quahog what they wanted to hear. I fed into their deep-rooted American fear and said whatever I knew would get them to dig into their pockets and fund my plan to clean up the lake. I discovered that all I had to do was make up some story about people wanting to kill us and say that I had some top-secret proof and voilà! **The money started flowin' in. I was able to clean up the lake and then . . . clean up.**

    I did some serious freakin' shopping while I was mayor. Holy crap! I would stay up until all hours of the night buying crap from the jewelry channel. Sapphires mostly 'cause I heard that's what Princess Diana was wearing when she died. I started an insane handbag collection, Coach, Balenciaga, Prada, Marc Jacobs, Gucci, Chanel, and a Birkin bag. I know that the way in which the purses came into my possession was wrong, but I WILL NOT return them. I would sooner light Meg on fire before having to part with my bags. **A good rule to remember: Don't mess with a woman's accessories.** (Especially a fat woman's, because accessories

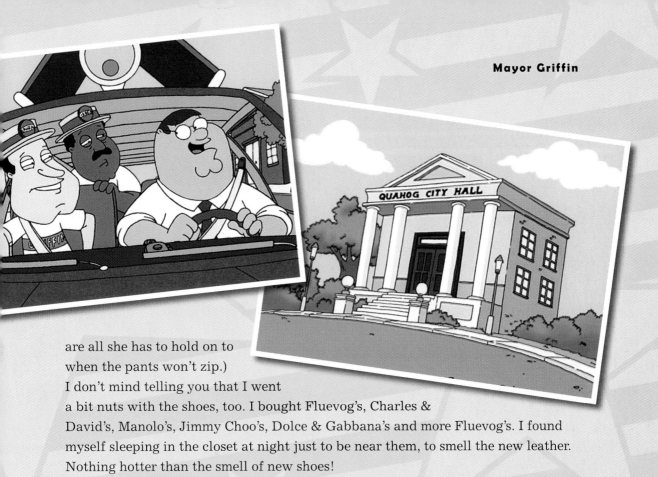

are all she has to hold on to
when the pants won't zip.)
I don't mind telling you that I went
a bit nuts with the shoes, too. I bought Fluevog's, Charles &
David's, Manolo's, Jimmy Choo's, Dolce & Gabbana's and more Fluevog's. I found
myself sleeping in the closet at night just to be near them, to smell the new leather.
Nothing hotter than the smell of new shoes!

The pièce-de-résistance from my disgusting, mayoral shopping spree is the fur
coat that ultimately led to my downfall. Now, I know many people

find fur to be a no-no in this very politically correct world that we live in, but I personally think it's a bunch of bull. **If I had a problem with fur coats, then I'd also have to have a problem with hot dogs and hamburgers and tennis shoes because they're all made from animals and you can't just protest killing the ones you think are cute.** That would be a bigger crime wouldn't it? To let the good-looking animals live while the ugly ones die? We would be living in a world of Aryan animals! A perfect animal race. Is that what we want? I think not. Sure it's awful to kill animals, but that's how the balance in nature works. After all, earthquakes, floods, and disease kill us. And let's not forget that every once in a while the animals have the last laugh, like that big tiger, Montecore, did with Roy Horn of Siegfried and Roy. I can't help but wonder if Montecore had been planning that attack for quite some time, or if it was just a whim. You know, maybe every night backstage before the show Montecore's conversation with the tiger in the next dressing room went something like this:

MONTECORE: I swear to God, if that dude gets in my face one more
time, I'm gonna—

TIGER #2: What? You're gonna what, Montecore?

MONTECORE: I'm going for the neck, man.

TIGER #2: Montecore, he's been treating you that way for years, and you always say that you're gonna leave him or fight back, and then the next thing I know, you're holding hands with him at the Christmas party.

MONTECORE: I know. I know. I just feel so fat lately and then I start believing that no one else will ever love me and before you know it—no, you know what? You're right. No more. Tonight's the night.

At any rate, that beautiful fur coat that I just had to have was the reason for my downfall. It was the key that opened my own evil "Pandora's Box." (**You know, I actually have "Pandora's Box" tattooed on my right inner thigh.**) I sold my soul to corporate America just so I could slip into those soft satin sleeves of comfort, and in doing so, I betrayed Quahog. I betrayed all of my friends and family. Everyone who worked so hard to put me in office. But most of all, I betrayed myself. I allowed big business to once again dump their waste in Lake Quahog. (And not the way that Peter or Chris would dump their waste in the lake. I'm talking toxic pollutants that could kill an elephant or Michael McDonald from the Doobie Brothers. Have you seen him lately? Boy did he blow up.) By committing such an egregious act, I became my parents. I became my father. I became sick to my stomach at the very thought of all the hard work that I'd undone with my selfishness.

But I am happy to report that there is a silver lining in all this. Even in the midst of corruption and scandal, I managed to grow the number of jobs in Quahog, raising the employment numbers for the first time in over a decade.

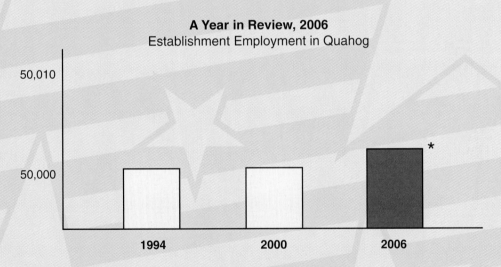

A Year in Review, 2006
Establishment Employment in Quahog

In 2006, Quahog employers added 1 job to the local economy according to new data released by the Department of Labor and Training's Labor Market Information Unit—the highest annual average on record in a decade!

* Year-over-year employment growth was first reported in the month after Mayor Pewterschmidt Griffin took office with the announcement that Brian Griffin was to be appointed as her Deputy Chief of Staff.

A Word from PETER

My wife, the mayor. Man, there is so much I want to tell you about what it was like for me, Peter Griffin, when my wife was in office. Unfortunately, I, Peter Griffin, am currently developing *My Wife, the Mayor* for ABC next fall, and they've asked that I not disclose any details about that time in our lives. But I can tell you that Lois was Mayor of Quahog, and Boss Hogg was Mayor of Hazzard County, so in essence, I, Peter Griffin was married to Boss Hogg. Incidentally, *The Dukes of Hazzard* was one of the best TV shows of all time. Here is a list of the other greatest freakin' shows and why they're so freakin' great:

1) *Matt Houston* (because he was like Magnum PI, but masculine.)
2) *Hart to Hart* (because when they met, it was murder.)
3) *Happy Days* (because it gave us our lord and savior, The Fonz. Amen.)
4) *Gilligan's Island* (because it was like a jerk-off sampler platter. There was someone for everyone on that little island.)
5) *Hogan's Heroes* (because Nazis = comedy.)
6) *The Hogan Family* (because Sandy Duncan = comedy. Love the episode where Sandy tries to quit smoking. So real.)
7) *CHiPs* (because Ponch was called Ponch. The best TV name ever!)
8) *Baywatch* (because the relationships and the characters were so real . . . nah! It's 'cause of the boobies.)
9) *Knight Rider* (because it must have been so much work to train that car to speak and do all those awesome tricks.)
10) *Dr. Quinn Medicine Woman* (because Jane Seymour's boobs were all covered up in her old time-y dresses so you really had to use your imagination. They really made you work for it.)

Before I, Peter Griffin, continue, I must tell you that I only agreed to take part in writing this book if HarperCollins promised to give me my own book deal, which they have. My book, due out next year, is entitled *The Definitive Guide to Living Large: A Fat Man's View from the Couch*. It's the book everyone wishes they had written—the one they can't believe no one else has written yet. **It will be the coffeetable book of choice in the home of every obese person across America (but you may not be able to see it under all the doughnut boxes and fast food wrappers).** It will include honest answers to such often asked questions as, "How do I go pee if I can't leave the couch?" and "Who will bring me the food that is slowly killing me?" I think it has a pretty good shot of making the *New York Times* bestseller list only because Amazon.com will deliver it right to these fat people's doorsteps. (God bless Amazon.com.) I'm working on the final two chapters right now, "When My Skin Fuses with the Couch Will I Become a Mythical Creature known as a Couchman?" and "How to Maintain a Healthy Relationship with the Neighbors Who Are Always Complaining That It Smells Like Dead Possums Over Here." Here's hoping this book strikes the chord that I think it will.

Hi, this is Peter writing again only I'm naked right now. I'm going over to the fridge now, but don't worry, I brought the paper and pen with me. I just got some pie out of the fridge. I'm eating pie with my left hand and writing with my right hand. **Now I'm wiping my sticky fingers on my butt cheek.** Lois just got home. She wants to know how come I didn't do any laundry. Now she's reading over my shoulder and giving me sort of a glar. She told me I spelled "glare" wrong. But now, down to business, here are three secrets about Lois that she doesn't want you to know:

1) She loves Q-tips. I don't mean that she just likes usin' 'em every now and then. I mean that she freakin' LOVES 'em! She likes to have one in each ear when we do it. An' when she's rollin' it around in her ear, her eyes roll back in her head a bit. It's kind of freaky and sometimes I get sad about it. Like, does she love the Q-tips more than me? Can I ever please her like the Q-tips do? I'll never know.

2) Lois leaves the toilet seat down all the freakin' time and it drives me nuts. Sometimes, in the middle of the night, I go in there to pee and it just gets all over the seat and when I sit down to pinch one off, I land right in my own pee-pee! It's disgusting and it hurts me that she just doesn't care enough to put the seat up when she's done.

3) On very hot summer days, Lois powders her private parts. In August, when it's really muggy, it looks like *Dangerous Liaisons* down there with all that freakin' white powder!

Oh, hey this is cool, here's a picture of me, nude, on the kitchen counter, waiting for toast.

When Lois was in office I did a lot of things that drove her nuts. For instance I would only refer to her as, "John Mayor Griffin," and I'd tell her that her body was a wonderland. I would also insist that she call me her "consigliere" and that she kiss my ring (after it had been down my pants). And one time I made her use my penis as the city's official letter opener. But there are a great many other things I did while Lois was in office that she still doesn't know about. I will tell you these things, if you swear you'll never tell her. Swear? Repeat after me, "I swear that I won't tell Lois about all the stuff Peter did when she was John Mayor Griffin. Amen. Lord, have mercy on my soul and tell Lance Bass that it's okay to be gay. Double amen."

Things I did while Lois was mayor that she still doesn't know about:

■ I shoplifted stuff (mostly candy from the Stop & Shop) and every time I ran into the store I yelled "By order of the queen!"

■ I farted on all the phones in City Hall. Every single one of 'em. It was a big job and it took forever, but it was hilarious.

■ I sat in as court stenographer one day and made it look like I was taking notes but I was really playing Tetris. Then I submitted random pages from old *Ranger Rick* and *Highlights* magazines instead of actual notes. Hehehehe. Goofus and Gallant are kick-ass!

■ I used scissors to cut slits in Lois's business skirts. I'd cut 'em about a $1/4$ inch higher every day so that by the end of two weeks you could see the promised land.

■ I secretly replaced all the straws in Quahog with swizzle sticks! A coupla people sucked so hard they had strokes . . . hilarious!

I farted on all the phones in City Hall.

■ I put Meg, Chris, and Stewie up for adoption. Then, as soon as someone was interested in them, I would cry and change my mind because it's the biological father's right to do so. (You should have seen the heartbroken looks on their faces.)

■ I accepted money from paparazzi photographers to shoot pictures of Stewie to be plastered all over *People* Magazine. I exploited my own flesh and blood out of greed and narcissism . . . just like most celebrity parents all over the world.

■ I reprogrammed all the digital scales at the gym to read ten pounds heavier. This sped up the deaths of at least six anorexic chicks so that other people could finally use the elliptical machines. I'm big on sharing.

Oh, and one more thing . . .
Do this on a calculator: "Dolly Parton went to the doctor in '69. (Press 69 on your calculator.) He said she had 2 boobs (press 2), 2 boobs (press 2) 2 many (press 2). He gave her 51 ways to cure it. (Press 51, then hit X.) She came back 8 weeks later (press 8, then =) and was left. . . . (Now turn the calculator upside down and read the answer: 55378008—upside down it looks like: "BOOBLESS.") Awesome, huh? Hehehehehehe.

A Word from STEWIE

Let's talk about death, shall we? Specifically, the death of a certain nasal-voiced, ginger-haired, meddlesome harpy of a woman that I am forced (damn you, biology!) to call Mother. For the longest time, indeed since birth, I've only wanted one thing—the death of Lois Griffin. Well, that and world domination. Well, that, and a signed Kelly Clarkson *Breakaway* CD, but I figure once I rule the world that should be pretty easy to come by. Call me, Kelly!

It is with a small (very small . . . one shouldn't get too down on oneself*) measure of regret that I write about my attempted, and sadly failed, assassination effort on Lois during her time in office as the mayor of this wretched city I call home. Due to circumstances beyond my control (how the devil was I supposed to know that the pudding cup Brian gave me would put me on a ten-minute sugar high followed immediately by a forty-minute nap?), my plan to shoot her multiple times in the head and neck during her inaugural parade did not go off exactly as I'd hoped. **But every experience is a learning experience† and besides, all the reading I did on famous assassinations and matricides in preparation for my attack will stay with me forever and will no doubt aid me in my future endeavors.** I learned what can go right, what can go wrong, and perhaps most importantly, what *not* to do . . . as you will see from the following examples.

> For the longest time, indeed since birth, I've only wanted one thing: the death of Lois Griffin.

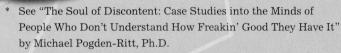

* See "The Soul of Discontent: Case Studies into the Minds of People Who Don't Understand How Freakin' Good They Have It" by Michael Pogden-Ritt, Ph.D.

† See "Once Bitten, Twice Shy: Learning How to Realize that Douchebags Don't Get Less Douchey the Longer You Date Them" by Leslie Amagrani, M.D., Ph.D.

1865: Abraham Lincoln, shot by John Wilkes Booth.
Nice job by Booth here—got Beardy McMoleFace right in the head from point-blank range. Of course, that was where the brilliant plan came to an abrupt halt. My God, breaking your own leg during your escape? How pathetic is that? And then getting yourself shot only a few weeks later? Hey, here's an idea, when you decide to kill someone, maybe try and live a little longer so that you can enjoy the results. Not really worth it otherwise, is it? Christ, what an amateur. We'll give him a 9.8 for the actual murder and a 2.0 for the follow-through.

1963: John F. Kennedy, shot by Lee Harvey Oswald.
Or was he? Need I say more with this one? If suspicion still abounds over forty years later as to whether or not you were the guy who actually did it, then you failed. Failed miserably. Look at Napoleon. Did he die of arsenic poisoning, or did he die of stomach cancer? Nobody knows. Nobody's sure. Maybe he *was* poisoned, but guess what, do we know who did it? Do we remember that guy's name? No. Same thing with Lee Harvey Oswald. Did he or didn't he? Was it him, or was it a giant conspiracy involving millions? My God, if you want to do something by committee and ensure that credit doesn't go to any one person, you might as well stay home and write a Nancy Drew novel. Oh, that's right, I said it—those much-beloved mysteries were written not by Carolyn Keene, but by a bunch of random authors-for-hire who didn't have enough clout to demand their own goddamn byline. Blew your mind, didn't I? Blew it and educated it, all at once.

1968: Martin Luther King Jr., shot by James Earl Ray.
See above. Conspiracy theory surrounding whether or not you were the one who actually killed the guy = you're a tool.

1980: John Lennon, shot by Mark David Chapman.
Catcher in the Rye, Mark? Really? Were you *trying* to make it obvious that you never got past a seventh-grade reading level? Did you think you were the only person ever in the whole wide world to be sad and disaffected? Did you think you were the first to discover that sometimes people are, oh, what's that so-very-original term . . . phony? Here's a thought: sometimes when people are depressed, they're unable to eat and therefore

they lose a bunch of weight. Think about that, you fat sack of useless.

Then there are the famous *attempted* assassinations, like good old John Hinckley trying to impress Jodie Foster by shooting at Ronald Reagan. First of all, John, you couldn't go Chapman-style and shoot the actual person you're obsessed with? You could have saved the entire planet from having to sit through *Nell*. Secondly, you nearly ended up shooting everyone *but* the guy you were aiming for. Come on. **Extra credit is fine and dandy, but you have to have gotten the *credit* first.** There are also the assassination attempts on Presidents Teddy and Franklin D. Roosevelt and Governor George Wallace, but guess what, those failed miserably, too. Who even remembers those? After all, nobody pays attention to things that don't work. Hear that, Tara Reid? It's over. It's been over. And the begging is embarrassing for everyone.

But on to matricide—an even better, and dare I say sexier, cousin to assassination. I can hardly lay claim to having come up with the brilliant idea of killing one's mother (billions of years ago there was no doubt a paramecium that divided in half, resulting in two smaller paramecia, one of which promptly killed the other), but I can certainly share what I've learned from past perpetrators. Let's take a look-see . . .

LIZZIE BORDEN

What *isn't* great about Lizzie Borden? Granted, she only hacked her stepmother and father 19 and 10 times respectively, not 40 and 41 like in the charming nursery rhyme*, but either way, well played, Lizzie, well played. And the best part of it all? She was acquitted! She was arrested, tried, and

---

* The original version of which went as follows: Lizzie Borden took an axe / Gave her mother nineteen whacks / When she saw what she had done / She thought to herself, "Wow, I should also kill my dad and then option the rights to my story for, like, a zillion bajillion dollars, and maybe even get my own reality TV show, because what's murder if you don't capitalize on it?" Note: the existence of this version of the rhyme is still in dispute.

then acquitted, and went on to live a perfectly happy, peaceful, and jail-free life! She was the O.J. Simpson of her time, and that, my friends, commands respect. She may have been a woman, but dear little Lizzie had balls of steel.

THE MENENDEZ BROTHERS

Okay, so these guys didn't escape nearly as scot-free as Lizzie did, but you know what, they got the job done, and that counts for something. So what if they went to jail—that hasn't stopped them from, say, getting married. Now, you might point out that they're not allowed conjugal visits, which means that they are both going to die in jail without ever banging their wives, but to this I say: the type of woman who is stupid enough to fall in love with a murderer who's in jail for life without parole is not the type of woman into which one would want to insert his phallus anyway. Not the brightest bulbs on the tree, those Menendez wives. Although I can sort of see where they're coming from— those boys aren't particularly difficult on the eyes.

You know, according to some people.

Especially in their cute little crewneck sweaters.

Not that it's relevant.

PRINCE WILLIAM and PRINCE HARRY

I know what you're going to say—Princess Diana was killed in a paparazzi-induced car accident. But did you ever stop to think about what it must have been like having a depressive, bulimic, adulterous bundle of neuroses for a mother? I mean, the woman threw herself down a flight of stairs during her first pregnancy—it's not exactly surprising that William, upon surviving this attempt at smashing the edges of a few dozen steps into his soft fetal head, might want to take a shot at some revenge. And perhaps Harry had a problem with the fact that all of Diana's pretty genes were apparently only strong enough to extend to one baby, leaving him with a bad case of Drew Lachey Syndrome. Or perhaps the two boys simply shared the opinion of many others and decided that anybody who would date a guy named Dodi deserves to die. Either way, conspiracy theories abound as to whether or not there were actually bombs that exploded that fateful night in that fateful car, and all I'm saying is hey, maybe point a finger at the kiddies. They've got money. They've got actual entitlement, instead of just a sense of it. They've got—oh, who am I kidding? That car accident was probably just an accident, and bless those two boys' hearts for being able to weather the tragedy of their mother's untimely death. How cool would it have been, though, if they had killed her? Pretty freakin' cool.

As you can see, I've learned much from the mistakes and successes of others. I've also learned from my own mistakes. After all, just as a relationship is not a failure simply because it ends (or so I've overheard Lois say every time she tries to talk one of her no-self-esteem friends down after their latest unceremonious dumping by a man who never cared in the first place), an attempted murder is not a failure simply because it failed to produce the death of the intended target. Okay, well, yes, it is, and that's why it's an attempted murder instead of an actual murder, but let's not get caught up in semantics. It'll only distract from the matter at hand, which is to examine the various attempts—dammit, there's that word again—I've made on Lois's life over the years. Starting with the womb, which was the site of my first try (and second, and third through sixth, actually) at killing Lois, and progressing through the months as I slowly gained the skills that come with each stage of infancy, here's a look at how I was able to tailor my attacks at each developmental level:

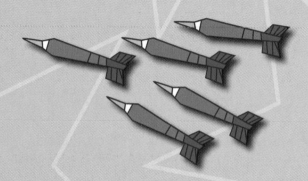

AGE (IN MONTHS)	MENTAL ABILITIES	PHYSICAL ABILITIES	SOCIAL ABILITIES	HOMICIDAL TECHNIQUES
1–2	Had only enough capacity to cry all the damn time.	Could do very little with my floppy neck and smushy head.	Could make eye contact; smiled, not that there was much to smile about.	Poisoning, because you can get maximum effect with minimal physical effort.
3–4	Learned cause and effect; understood that things have names, like "dog" or "fat man."	Could sit; could stand as long as someone helped. (Thanks, Rupert!)	Laughed, assuming something was actually funny; could tell difference between parents and strangers and, accordingly, treat strangers better.	Knives; it's better to work close-range when your aim isn't that great yet.
5–6	Acquired interest in colors, objects, colored objects.	Rolled over; crawled in a lame, gimpy way.	Babbled; watched mouths to mimic sounds and the occasional naughty word.	Crossbow, because a manual bow and arrow is for pussies.
7–9	Began to understand physical concepts like "behind" or "inside" (not in a sexual way, you pervert).	Drank from cup (yum, juice); fed self (yum, Cheerios); picked up small objects (yum, carpet lint).	Exhibited various changes of mood; responded to name (Stewie, Mr. Griffin if you're nasty).	Handguns, now that I had the motor skills to quickly reload.
10–12	Understood phrases; occasionally pretended not to in order to avoid accountability.	Crawled efficiently; walked with help, (Hey, the fat man is good for *something*).	Learned to enjoy games and say simple words ("damn," "you," "vile," "woman," etc.).	Throwing stars, machetes, machine guns, hunting knives, booby-trapped household objects—you name it, I've got it, and Lois is on the other end of it.

And now that I'm a fully capable one-year-old, I'm able to strategize murder attempts in ever more complicated ways. For example, here's the schematic of my assassination plans for Lois during her inaugural parade.

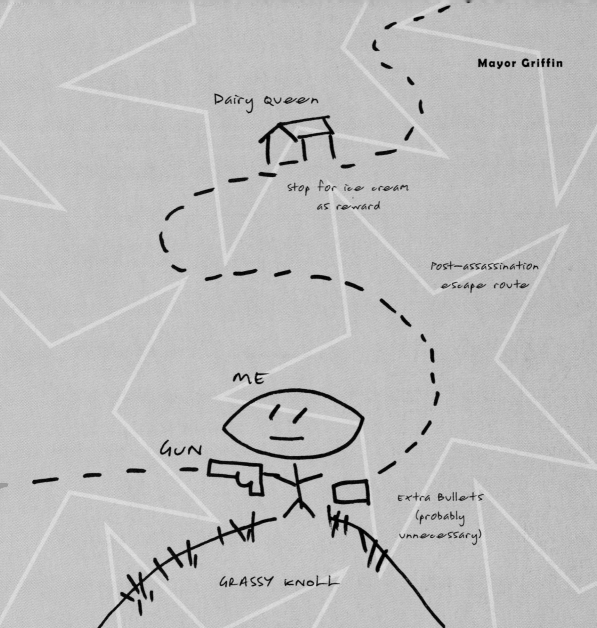

Dairy Queen

Stop for ice cream
as reward

Post-assassination
escape route

ME

GUN

Extra Bullets
(probably
unnecessary)

GRASSY KNOLL

Well, I hope this review of my homicidal tendencies and efforts has been as enjoyable and enlightening for you as it has been for me, although if it hasn't, I could give a crap. As is probably obvious, I have not yet succeeded in killing Lois. But don't worry, her death will come someday. I promise you that.

Bitch gonna get it.

Epilogue
by Brian Griffin

Like a fine single malt scotch, Lois Pewterschmidt Griffin has only gotten better with age. While the ephemeral bloom of her youth may have faded ever-so-slightly over the years, her intelligence, passion, and capabilities have grown by leaps and bounds. She remains a vital, exuberant, infinitely patient woman with the ability not only to conceive plans to make the world a better place, but to implement those plans. **In short, she is the kind of leader this country has been lacking.** The kind of leader we're in desperate, desperate need of. The kind that I and millions of like-minded individuals are determined to elect again one day.

During her brief, yet effective tenure as mayor, Lois made more improvements to the city of Quahog than this nation has seen on a federal or state level since the (stolen) election of 2000,* and she truly is a living illustration of the positive change that can be effected when informed, thoughtful citizens—or even just a lone nasal-yet-comforting voice—care enough to spearhead it.

Especially today, when we are saddled with a government that continues to run roughshod over the desires of what is clearly the majority of the population†, it's refreshing to see a woman who knew what she wanted to accomplish from the very

---

* See *Bush v. Gore*. Supreme Court of the United States on Writ of Certiorari to the Florida Supreme Court, Dec. 12, 2000. Also known as "The Beginning of the End."

† See "The President's Approval Rating: Falling Faster than Kirsten Dunst's Boobs," page 35.

first moment she set foot in office, and, unlike some people,* worked tirelessly to achieve those goals. Despite continuing her duties as wife, mother, and practical leader of the Griffin household, Lois managed to tackle many issues in Quahog that are also nationwide problems currently being either ignored or worsened by the incompetents on Capitol Hill. A few brief examples:

THE ENVIRONMENT.   While the current administration handles global warming with a "close your eyes and maybe it'll go away, if it's even really happening, which we say it's not" strategy, Lois, mere weeks after being sworn into office, stopped the dumping of toxic waste into Lake Quahog. She kicked off the celebration of its new pollution-free waters by taking the inaugural swim, for which she wore a white bikini.

A *white* bikini.

And the water was cold.

Think about it.

THE PUBLIC EDUCATION SYSTEM.   While "No Child Left Behind" in practice leaves more children behind than a deadbeat dad[†], Lois committed fully to improving the public schools of Quahog, levying a new tax that affected only the very wealthy in order to fund supplemental reading and science programs for students K-12. She also helped out on a personal level, doing her best to encourage reading among children by volunteering at the library's Story Hour. I went once, just to listen to her voice, which is so soothing. You can just hear it whispering naughty things—when she was talking about the little engine that could, my little engine definitely could. (By that I mean my penis.)

WOMEN'S RIGHTS AND SEX EDUCATION.   While the conservatives of our government continue their quest to enslave women (and for that matter, men) with unnecessary legislation regarding personal and private rights, Lois made it her

---

* See "Vacations Are Better Than Working, So There! And Also Coloring Is Fun, and Also Puppies" by George W. Bush, page 4.
† See "Four Kids? What's Your Point? There's Weed I Gots to Smoke" by Kevin Federline, page 7.

business to put condoms in the schools and open extra Planned Parenthood clinics throughout town. She even toyed with instituting a "nine abortions get the tenth one free" punchcard policy, but as it turns out this never even became an issue, thanks to the multitude of safe and effective birth control methods Lois made it her business to educate the entire city about. You haven't known happiness until you've seen Lois wearing a power suit and stiletto heels while demonstrating the proper use of a dental dam.

God is she hot. She's so. Smoking. Hot. The things I would do to her, given the chance . . .

Where was I? Oh yeah, uh, political stuff. Let's see . . .

UM. FEARMONGERING ABOUT TERRORISM. Yeah. The government's really into that. Which is both hypocritical—considering all the information they are purposely withholding from the populace*—and just plain evil on various and sundry levels. Look at the NSA's illegal wiretapping of innocent citizens' phone conversations. I mean, Lois would never do that. She would never, ever listen on the phone to someone else's private exchange, except for that one time when Peter thought it would be hot to have her on the line while he called a phone sex worker.† Yeah, he told me about it. At first I was painfully and uncontrollably aroused at this clear demonstration that Lois has no problem with experimentation regarding the bedroom, and then I was overwhelmed by a violent feeling of jealousy and disbelief that a vibrant, sexy, worldly, fiercely intelligent woman with an ass that won't quit would marry and stay married to a guy who names his farts. It's maddening! It's beyond infuriating! It's . . .

Um, back to the good things that Lois did for Quahog during her tenure as mayor, one of which was the maintenance and beautification of the public parks system. Lois is all about keeping trees pruned, lawns under control, and bushes trimmed. Bushes trimmed. I'm just saying.

Plus, Lois didn't kill thousands of innocent people by starting a pointless war,

---

* See "You Think 9/11 Is The First Thing We Lied About? Bitch, Please" by Prick Dick Cheney, page 52.

† See *Freaktastic Things My Wife Has Done That I Bet Your Wife Wouldn't Do*, Chapter 6: "Stuff Involving Phones and/or Other Electronic Objects and Equipment," by Peter Griffin.

which, you know, would kinda put her ahead in my book if she weren't already so far ahead anyway. Oh my God, I want her so bad. You don't even understand. I love her so much. I would do anything for her. Here's a letter I wrote to her once in one of my many moments of weakness:

Dear Lois,

I'm sorry, but I just can't go on this way any longer. You have to know the truth. . . . I owe that much to both of us. Please read this all the way through, and please try to understand.

When you pet me, it sends shivers down my spine. Sometimes I want to hump your leg so badly I start crying.

Sometimes when you come home from shopping, it's all I can do not to go sprinting up to the door as you walk in and then jump up and down next to you the entire time you're trying to put away the groceries.

Whenever you bring me a soup bone, all I think about is how much I want to bone you.

If you ever passed out on the floor and stayed unconscious for hours, I would absolutely not chew your face off like that Labrador did to that French chick who ended up getting the face transplant.

What I'm trying to say is that I love you. It has to be said, after all these years we've known each other and all the scotch I just drank.

I love you. I love you, Lois. Oh my God, I love you so much. I love you.

Your humble servant, always and forever,

Brian

P.S. I've included a MASH note that proves we were meant to be together!

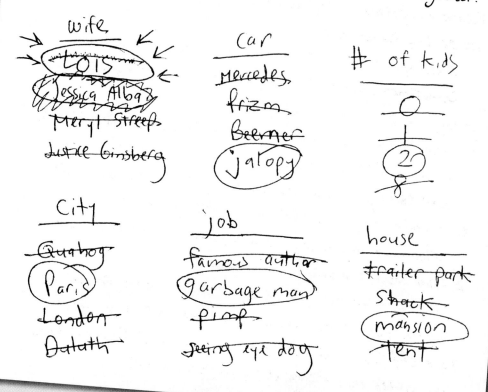

wife
- ~~LOIS~~
- ~~Jessica Alba~~
- ~~Meryl Streep~~
- ~~Justice Ginsberg~~

car
- ~~Mercedes~~
- ~~Prizm~~
- ~~Beemer~~
- (jalopy)

# of kids
- 0
- ~~1~~
- (2)
- ~~8~~

City
- ~~Quahog~~
- (Paris)
- ~~London~~
- ~~Duluth~~

job
- ~~famous author~~
- (garbage man)
- ~~pimp~~
- ~~seeing eye dog~~

house
- ~~trailer park~~
- ~~shack~~
- (mansion)
- ~~tent~~

June 15, 2006

Dear HarperCollins,

I recently submitted a manuscript for the epilogue of *It Takes a Village Idiot . . . and I Married One!* by Lois Griffin. Please be advised that I mistakenly included a handwritten letter beginning "Dear Lois" in my submission and that I would now like to request retraction of that letter. Please return the original to me and delete it from the book's final text.

I apologize for any inconvenience or publishing delay I may have caused. Your prompt action is greatly appreciated. Thank you very much.

Sincerely yours,

Brian

Brian Griffin

June 16, 2006

Dear HarperCollins,

I recently wrote to you regarding the retraction of a letter I submitted for *It Takes a Village Idiot . . . and I Married One!* by Lois Griffin. Please disregard my previous letter (dated June 15, 2006) and continue with the printing of the original letter that begins "Dear Lois." There's no reason that Lois, Peter, and the whole world shouldn't know that I'm madly in love with her.

Thank you very much.

Sincerely yours,

Brian

Brian Griffin

June 17, 2006

Dear HarperCollins,

Please disregard my letter to you dated June 16, 2006. I would appreciate it if you would delete the "Dear Lois" letter from the final manuscript of *It Takes a Village Idiot . . . and I Married One!*, return the original to me, and forget anything ever happened. Thank you.

Sincerely yours,

Brian

Brian Griffin

Puzzle Answers

ANAGRAMS

An anagram of Lois Griffin: "If girl, if son"

An anagram of Lois Pewterschmidt Griffin: "Limp wristed if strong chief."

Acknowledgments and Dedications

For giving me their undying support and encouragement, I'd like to thank my wonderful husband, Peter, and my beautiful children, Chris and Stewie. Oh, and Meg. Each one of you has occupied my vagina at one time or another, and I treasure every one of those memories. (Some more than others, of course. For the record, I much prefer my vagina's use as an entrance.) —LPG

I would like to take this opportunity to thank my parents for having had sexual relations that led to my birth. I'd also like to thank them for never spanking me, or making me go to bed at any particular time. Their total "hands-off" approach made me the foul-mouthed insomniac that I am, and without those qualities, this book might not exist. So thank you, Mom and Dad. I'd also like to thank my husband, Jackson, for picking up my parents' slack by spanking me constantly.

This may not be the appropriate time or place, but I would like to ask Cherry to pay me back the five bucks she borrowed from me that one day while we were working on this book. Remember? You said, "Oh, I'll pay you tomorrow," and you never did. You see, Cherry is the kind of person who always says she'll do a lot of things, but then doesn't. She's kind of a lying bitch. The truth is, that I'm really glad that this book is finally finished so I never have to look at her stupid, bitch face again. Oh, and by the way, Cherry . . . I DO know what an adverb is!

Example: Cherry acted so cunty most of the time, but what do you expect?

She is, after all, a cunt. Oh, and speaking of cunts, I'd also like to dedicate this book to my Grandma Nagy, who did not live to see its publication. *Szeretlek!* —AB

I did pay Alex, but her dog ate it. So Alex, you should be getting that five bucks back some time very soon. Hope it's "Pepper-y" enough for you. By the way, can you pet Pepper for me? He or she is really cute and I feel like I've gotten to know him or her really well.

Thanks to Hope Innelli, Debbie Olshan, Wendell Riggins, Sharon Ross, Carl A. Braxton, and the writing staff of *Family Guy*. Every one of you is devastatingly sexy. And of course, thanks to Seth MacFarlane. Because he's the sexiest. —CC

Cherry said that we would thank Hope, Debbie, Wendell, Sharon, Carl, all the writers, and Seth together, but then she just went ahead and thanked them herself. Do you see what I had to deal with? —AB